Always With You
I AM

A short story of encouragement
for little children

By Kathryn Rae

Cover Illustrations by Rae
Interior Illustrations by Rae, Mason and Kathryn Rae

WestBow Press books may be ordered through booksellers or by contacting:

WestBow Press
A Division of Thomas Nelson
1663 Liberty Drive
Bloomington, IN 47403
www.westbowpress.com
1-(866) 928-1240

ISBN: 978-1-4497-4202-7 (sc)

Library of Congress Control Number: 2012903902

Printed in the United States of America

WestBow Press rev. date: 04/05/2012

WestBow
PRESS
A DIVISION OF THOMAS NELSON

This book is dedicated
to all the children in the world.

"Be sure of this; I am with you always,
even until the end of time".
-Matthew 28:20

I am always with you.
I AM
I am with you while you are sleeping.
I am with you when you are awake.
I am with you when you are
playing in the sunshine.
I am with you when you are
playing in the rain.
I am always with you.
I AM

I love you.
YOU are special.
I made you just like ME.

I made
the sunshine,
the rain,
the moon,
the stars,
Venus and Mars.

I made all of the animals
for you to enjoy.
I made the itzy bitzy lady bug,
the floppy eared elephant,
the long neck giraffe
and the slug.

I made all of the fish
swimming in the sea
and all of the
birds flying high
In the sky.

Look! Look!
Do you see the bees?
They are playing and
buzzing in the breeze.

Look up!
What do we see?
Birds flying high.
Birds flying way up
high above the trees.

I made them
for you
and for me.

But most of all,
after I made the
sunshine and the rain,

the moon and the stars,
Venus and Mars,
the itzy bitzy lady bug,
the floppy eared elephants,

the long
neck giraffe
and the slug,

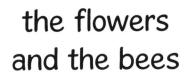
the flowers
and the bees

and the fish
that swim and play
in the sea,

I made you
just like me.
Just like me.
I AM

Thank you God
for Your great love
and thank you God
for sending us The Dove.
Amen.

Printed in the United States
By Bookmasters